LYDIA

The Woman You Must Know

Maame Grace

Order this book online at www.trafford.com
or email orders@trafford.com

Most Trafford titles are also available at major online book retailers.

Unless otherwise noted, all scripture quotations are from the NIV Study Bible

Printed in Victoria, BC, Canada.

ISBN: 978-1-4251-2086-3

*Our mission is to efficiently provide the world's finest, most comprehensive book publishing
service, enabling every author to experience success. To find out how to publish your
book, your way, and have it available worldwide, visit us online at www.trafford.com*

Trafford rev. 3/8/10

 www.trafford.com

North America & international
toll-free: 1 888 232 4444 (USA & Canada)
phone: 250 383 6864 ♦ fax: 812 355 4082

To my lovely daughters, Gracie and Joshi

my babies in Christ and

my beloved single mothers

who are aspiring to be the women God created them to be

FOREWORD

This interesting and must read book comes in handy at a time when women all over the world are reclaiming their place in society. Especially, in terms of their status at home and outside the home. For the woman who fears God; reading this book will be an exciting addition to this experience.

I have known the author, since she was a young woman. Grace had always desired to be a servant of God as she modeled her life after *Lydia*, the Thyatirian woman she presents in this book. Grace always seeks to influence young women to do the same.

I worked with the author from the late 1980's to the early 1990s in the Baptist Women's Ministry, Ghana. She became the National President of the Young Ladies Association (Lydia), during this time when I was then, the National President of the Women's Ministry.

I had the opportunity to mentor this wonderful woman whose desire was to win souls; especially, young ladies for God and motivate them to use their potential. With humor and sincerity, Grace always made time out of her busy schedule to share her life with these young ladies.

Grace had often expressed that she wanted to put down her thoughts about this biblical character, *Lydia*. And in many times, her vision and ambition had been thwarted. At last she has done it by the grace of God.

I find this book very interesting and timely to address contemporary issues which she might not have taken care off if she had published it earlier. I am therefore not surprised that after so many years, her dream of helping Christian women in this way has finally been fulfilled.

I am glad to invite you; career women, single mothers and young women. Also, Pastors, Lay Preachers and Church Leaders (who seek to promote the well-being of women). And all Christians, who seek to bring others to the saving knowledge of Jesus Christ, to read this book.

You will find answers to your questions as you face the realities of your own ideas of fulfillment and empowerment.

Juliana Gyanwa Adu- Gyamfi, (Mrs)
November, 2009

PREFACE

I have always wanted to write a book about Lydia. This is my third attempt and I thank God for its completion.

My interest in Lydia began in my late teens when I joined a Christian Young Women's group called *Lydia* in the Grace Baptist Church, Kumasi, Ghana. The Lydia group was the youth wing of the Women's Missionary Union (W.M.U.) of the Ghana Baptist Convention. Lydia members were mostly teenagers and young adults, who were students, professionals, business women or apprentices of trade and unmarried. And in fact, the group was designed for single young women in the church. The regular W.M.U. membership was mostly adult, married, women. The two groups focused on different things. W.M.U. members focused on married life and parenting, whiles Lydia members were concerned with developing a career, and Christian courtship.

I served as the Lydia national director in the late 1980s to early 1990s. My passion for the members at the time was to see young women empowered by the Holy Spirit to serve Christ, and maximize their potential to be the women God created them to be.

I wrote my first *Lydia* manuscript in 1989. The manuscript was proof-read and type-setted but never got printed. It eventually got lost. I tried another time with no success. But I kept the research notes and nurtured the hope to rewrite it someday.

My life has changed considerably since I wrote the first manuscript. Though I regret that it was not published in those days, I thank God, for preventing it until now.

Almost 20 years after the first manuscript, I have suddenly developed interest to complete the book. By the grace of God, my scope has broadened in terms of issues relating to Lydia as a woman, which was not explored in the previous manuscripts. I have also developed through diverse life experiences. And I believe, these experiences have contributed to enrich the content of this book.

Lydia: the woman you must know is a character study of the New Testament woman, Lydia. The book contains historical and secular information to help explain the biblical text. With the exception of Bible quotations, there are no citations from other sources. I have put some words in *italics* for emphasis. My sources of information are all listed under bibliography at the end of the book. I took this approach to present the book for easy reading.

Divided into two parts, the book presents Lydia as the New Testament woman who lived like any independent successful modern woman. The book also shed light on the Apostle Paul's missionary work in Europe and the challenge he faced in starting the European missions with a woman as his main contact. Paul had no choice but to work with Lydia and her friends who were devoted to God. The success of Paul's work produced the first Christian church in Europe at Philippi.

Other subjects that are treated in the book are; the Christian discipline of waiting, how to become a "born again" Christian, how to lead family members to Christ, and how to realise your dreams through systematic planning and determination to complete set goals.

Under the unique qualities of Lydia in the part two of the book, I have attempted to show the abstract concept of God-fearing in the everyday practical life of the Christian woman,

Lydia. As an ideal woman, Lydia's devotion to God and her successful, independent character provides an example for the Christian woman of today. Her unique qualities are crowned in the discussion of Lydia as the example of a liberated God-fearing woman.

Lydia: the woman you must know is not an academic book. It is one God-fearing woman's quest to bring meaning to the idea of living as a Christian liberated woman in today's world. The book is also a celebration of my personal experience of practical walk with the Lord Jesus Christ.

My scope on the issues discussed in the book results from group and personal Bible studies, literature reviews, sermons from the pulpit, fellowship with other believers, Bible school lectures and every day life experiences.

What follows therefore, is a condensed work of how God taught me vital lessons in life as a liberated Christian woman through the biblical character, Lydia.

As you begin to read this book, may God bring home to you, the desire to aspire to reach the potential He (God) created you to be.

ACKNOWLEDGEMENT

I thank God for helping me to write this book. I thank Him for my parents, especially my late father who taught me that names are significant and I must live up to my name. May he rest in peace.

Special thanks to my husband Chris, who allows me to be the woman God created me to be. He had never ceased to encourage me to pursue my dreams since the first day I met him.

I thank my children Chris Jnr., Gracie and Joshi for their support. They understand when to leave "mommy" alone so that she can work.

I thank pastor Alex Lappos for reviving my desire to write again.

Special thanks to all my friends for their support. Specifically, Lydia Rousseau who kept pestering me to complete the book, from the first day that I told her I was writing about her name sake. Cynthia Garçon, Hawa Conteh and Eden Verzosa.

Pastor Sarah Buttler, Sister Reada Tucker, Inica, Patricia Christopher, Patience Dzandzu and Ursula Bastien, are but a few of the God-fearing women who helped me in different ways. I thank my colleague Gina Carvalho for her criticism and editorial support.

Special thanks to Mrs. Juliana Adu-Gyamfi, a woman that I have always admired as a model liberated Christian woman. She provided enormous help from Ghana through emails and telephone calls. And offered constructive criticisms that helped reshape the book for better reading. She also took time off from her busy schedule to write the foreword.

Finally, I thank Angela Aidoo for providing editorial services, Mike Bennet for designing the inspiring book cover and the staff at Trafford Publishing.

Table of Contents

Lydia's story appears in the New Testament passage in Acts 16:6-15 and 40

*P*aul and his companions traveled throughout the region of Phrygia and Galatia, having been kept by the Holy Spirit from preaching the word in the province of Asia. When they came to the border of Mysia, they tried to enter Bithynia, but the Spirit of Jesus would not allow them to. So they passed by Mysia and went down to Troas. During the night Paul had a vision of a man of Macedonia standing and begging him, "Come over to Macedonia and help us." After Paul had seen the vision, we got ready at once to leave for Macedonia, concluding that God had called us to preach the gospel to them. From Troas we put out to sea and sailed straight for Samothrace, and the next day on to Neapolis. From there we traveled to Philippi, a Roman colony and the leading city of that district of Macedonia. And we stayed there several days.

On the Sabbath we went outside the city gate to the river, where we expected to find a place of prayer. We sat down and began to speak to the women who had gathered there. One of those listening was a woman named Lydia, a dealer in purple cloth from the city of Thyatira, who was a worshiper of God. The Lord opened her heart to respond to Paul's message. When she and the members of her household were baptized, she invited us to her home. "If you consider me a believer in the Lord," she said, "come and stay at my house." And she persuaded us.

After Paul and Silas came out of the prison, they went to Lydia's house, where they met with the brothers and encouraged them. Then they left.

PART ONE

THE WOMAN LYDIA

One of those listening was a woman named Lydia, a dealer in purple cloth from the city of Thyatira.

Acts 16:14

CHAPTER ONE

THE WOMAN CALLED LYDIA

This is the story of a woman called Lydia who lived in the early days of the Christian faith.

Lydia was the first Christian convert in Europe. She was popular among the early Christians in Europe as a kind, independent and successful woman.

Lydia was neither a minister nor a church leader. She was just a woman who had strong faith in God and decided to live her life to please Him. And by so doing, Lydia affected many people's lives in a way she never dreamt of, and left posterity with a successful story that every woman must know.

The story of Lydia took place over 2000 years ago and so it is history. Unlike any other historic account, Lydia's story is a kind of history about love.

It is a history of a woman's love for her God.

And a history of a God-fearing, independent woman who lived a liberated life in a male-dominated culture before the concept of women's liberation was born.

Lydia's story was briefly told in the New Testament book of Acts of the Apostles chapter 16, but few people know about it. Although the story of Lydia is recorded in the New Testament, it is secular history outside the New Testament that provides the rich insight and understanding into the simple Bible story.

In this book, Lydia's story is augmented with information from sources other than the Bible that relates to the times and the culture she lived in. Readers are encouraged to reflect on her story.

I hereby invite you to get acquainted with this New Testament woman, who brings her unique woman's contribution to Christianity today.

She was a Lydian

Lydia's name derived from her origins. Her home region was known as the Kingdom of Lydia. In those days, her name Lydia could simply mean a woman from the Kingdom of Lydia.

The ancient Kingdom of Lydia was known to be a very wealthy kingdom, and it covered parts of Asia Minor. Historians have indicated that the Kingdom of Lydia was the first nation to make coins.

There were famous kings from the kingdom including King Croesus who was known in history as the richest king of his time. He was so rich that he spawned the simile: *as rich as Croesus.* The name: Kingdom of Lydia outlived its time. During the New Testament times, the kingdom became a province of the Roman Empire but it continued to be known as the Kingdom of Lydia.

Lydia came from the town of Thyatira which was in the Kingdom of Lydia. Thyatira would be around modern day Turkey. It was a prosperous commercial city with different types of trades including the purple dye business.

In the book of Revelations, an assembly of Christian believers in Thyatira was mentioned as one of the seven churches that received a letter from the Apostle John (Revelation 2:18-29).

Because Lydia's name was the same as the Kingdom of Lydia some Bible teachers believe that "Lydia" was not her real name but as noted earlier, a reference to a Lydian. Consequently, they assume that Lydia could have been one of the women called Euodia or Syntyche whom Paul mentioned as members in the church of Philippi (Philippians 4:2).

Lydia lived in Philippi

Lydia was living in Philippi in the European region of Macedonia when she converted into the Christian faith. Philippi would be in modern day Greece.

The city was named after King Phillip II, the father of Alexander the Great who named the town after himself when he conquered the region.

Philippi was a Roman colony city, so it received special treatment in the Roman Empire. The city had its own government fashioned after that of Rome, the capital of the empire. Philippi was also directly accountable to Rome and did not pay taxes to the Macedonian government.

One of the advantages in living in colony cities was that people were granted Roman citizenships despite the fact that they lived away from Rome. Paul for example, was a Roman citizen, although he had Jewish parents and lived in Tarsus (Acts16:37; 22:25-28).

Philippi had a commercial advantage because it was situated in the major highway called *Via Egnatia* that connected the eastern provinces of the Roman Empire to the capital Rome and the western provinces.

The Roman Empire at that time covered Britain, Spain, Portugal, France and Germany on the western side (although the area was then known as Gaul). On the eastern side, it stretched across Greece to the western parts of Asia, Palestine and also parts of North Africa.

All business in the empire ended in Rome as the saying: *all roads lead to Rome.*

Historians agree on the pomposity of the Philippian citizens because of their privileged position in the empire. They copied the Roman lifestyle: men wore togas—a garment that only a full citizen of Rome was permitted to wear—and women, the loosely fitting gowns and hair styles of the contemporary Roman women.

In addition to the clothing, several Philippian nobles spoke flawless Latin—which was the official Roman language—and enjoyed past times in the amphitheatres and acropolis. They also worshiped different deities and considered the Roman emperor Caesar as divine. Partying, loose sexual lifestyle, slavery and the low regard for the poor in society were some of the Roman cultural values also practiced in Philippi.

But from what was written about Lydia in the Bible, her main attraction would not be to adapt to this Philippian lifestyle. She rose above that copious (Roman) culture, focused on pleasing God and humbly sought a better citizenship in the Kingdom of God. Relying on her unwavering faith in God, Lydia was shaped into a woman of success as she lived in Philippi.

Lydia was an immigrant

It's interesting that the writer of the New Testament story needed to mention the fact that Lydia was a native of Thyatira and not Philippi where she was comfortably living as a business woman. This would suggest that there was something significant about her status as an immigrant woman.

Many immigrants identify mostly with their new country other than their native one not to cast a slur on their home country but in order to benefit from resources that they would otherwise be denied. For example, access to free education, medicals, child support, and the ability to own property.

Lydia's immigrant experience cannot be ruled out when trying to understand her successful story.

No reason was given for why she moved from Thyatira to Philippi. But I would not rule out a search for a better life even if she had followed parents, husband or friends.

I too am an immigrant woman who grew up mostly in my country of origin before I moved abroad. I know how difficult it is to adjust to life in a new country.

Everything is different! The food, weather, culture, even the language if the same can have different meaning!

For an example: you go to a restaurant and order a chicken and rice dish expecting a seasoned roasted chunk of chicken on a salted bed of cooked rice. Only to be served with a tasteless, skinless, white piece of chicken in a broth. Trimmed of all fat for health reasons and served on a spoonful of tasteless cooked rice.

You dress in your best cotton dress and to go out only to realise that what you are wearing could barely stand the cold temperature outside. Raising your voice in expressive language to a neighbour maybe considered bizarre and to your child can end you behind bars for a day or two. Above these are the encompassing differences in language and accent that can become a barrier to communication and social mobility.

These examples are but a few of the daily realities of the immigrant life.

Many immigrants break down in the process of adapting into life in the new country. And families break down. At this stage, usually *things fall apart, and the centre cannot hold.*

It is often at this stage that many make compromises and sacrifices that either help them or place them in a situation contrary to all the values they learnt in life. The risk to forgo beliefs, values, and practices held dear is high.

Certainly, Lydia was not exempted from these immigrant experiences but survived and proved that God-fearing women have what it takes to meet these challenges.

She remained the Lydian woman she was raised to be and won the accolade the *woman from Thyatira.* How she did it, is what this book is about.

Reflect on these:

1. What is your name? Check the meaning of your name and see if you are living up to it.

2. List things from your childhood that you still cherish as important for your life today.

3. Sketch your identity now and reflect on things that you do not hold important in your life anymore. Why do you not value them anymore?

4. Does leaving behind some things from your background make you a better person or not?

Charm is deceptive, and beauty is fleeting; but a woman who fears the LORD is to be praised.

Proverbs 31:30

CHAPTER TWO

LYDIA FEARED GOD

Of all the titles in the world, none is as prestigious to me as "a woman who fears God."

Lydia's story is about a woman who remarkably held this title. Lydia maintained faith in God with such a passion that nothing in the ungodly society she lived in at Philippi could shake her.

People did not believe in a one true God just as today where many claim to be unbelievers in the existence of God. People prefer to turn to caring for nature, volunteering in the community or being kind to strangers to satisfy their conscience for a better world. But none of these acts make faith in God a fallacy.

We Christians believe that there is God. To us, God is the creator of the universe, the One and Only True God of the Bible. He is the same God many refer to as the God of Israel, and also the God of all those who believe in Jesus Christ as Lord and Saviour.

Lydia knew this God even before she became a Christian.

How was this possible, you may ask?

Lydia likely knew and worshipped Him in her native Thyatira, before she moved to Philippi. Or else her parents who knew this God of Israel made sure she knew Him when she was growing up. And that knowledge of God became a package of Lydia's upbringing which she never threw away.

The Bible described Lydia as a *Worshipper of God* which is also translated as *God-fearer* in some Bible versions.

I am using The New International Version (NIV) of the Bible for quotations in this book and in it the translation *Worshipper of God* is used to describe Lydia. So I will explain what it means to be a *Worshipper of God* as I attempt to discuss what it means to *fear God*.

Worshipper of God-what is it?

When the Bible referred to Lydia as a *Worshipper of God* it implied that Lydia was an adherent to the Jewish religion (Judaism). The title *Worshipper of God*, described non-Jewish converts to Judaism.

Cornelius, the Roman soldier in Acts chapter 10 and the Ethiopian eunuch in Acts chapter 8:27 were two examples of gentile *Worshippers of God*. None of them was born Jewish, but they loved the God of Israel and sought after Him.

While the Eunuch, an African courtier, travelled all the way from the southern Kingdom of Ethiopia to Jerusalem to worship God, the Roman centurion eagerly followed the regular devotional times of the God of the people he had conquered.

One common thing among this *Worshippers of God* was their eagerness to observe Jewish religious rituals; that is Jewish holidays, prayer times, feasts and dietary restrictions.

For example, the Ethiopian Eunuch attended a feast in Jerusalem (Acts 8:27). And Cornelius maintained regular prayer times and gave generously to those in need (Acts 10:2).

Lydia and the women by the Philippian riverside were also observing the Sabbath day (Acts 16:13-14).

Worshippers of God were among the first people to accept the gospel in the early days when Christianity was preached to the gentile world. Cornelius, the Ethiopian Eunuch, and Lydia are examples of these in the Bible.

Now we have laid the background to the fact that Lydia knew about the God of Israel and sought to worship Him. But the next question will be how did she get to know this God being a Lydian from Thyatira?

Lydia knew God

I believe Lydia developed faith in the God of Israel when she was living in Thyatira and long before she moved to Philippi. My reason is mostly based on history and the Bible story about Lydia.

During the reign of the wealthy King Croesus, the Kingdom of Lydia was conquered by the Persians whose military strategy included resettling conquered peoples. At the time, the Persians resettled the conquered Jewish people to different parts of their empire, possibly to prevent local uprisings. Some Jews were resettled in the Kingdom of Lydia.

It is known in history, and even at present, that Jewish people practice their religion and culture wherever they live. Their high moral standards of life might have attracted people in the Lydian Kingdom. And in Thyatira, those who were attracted might have included Lydia and her family.

Several Jewish people lived in the ancient Kingdom of Lydia and by the New Testament times there were several Jewish communities in several Asian towns. That is why in the New Testament, especially in the book of Acts there were mentions of Jewish synagogues where Paul preached.

Since the Jewish religion and culture was practiced by those attracted to it, Lydia immersed herself completely in it and practiced her new religion with such zeal that her lifestyle resembled that of a Jewish girl.

I was not surprised during my research when I came across materials that described Lydia as a Jewish girl who converted into Christianity. I knew it was not true because the Bible clearly states that, Lydia was a *Worshipper of God*. But I was thrilled by the implication that writers thought she was Jewish because of her devotion to the Jewish God.

Lydia's risky choice to fear God

Worshipping a Jewish God in Roman Philippi might not be the best choice and risky at the time for Lydia.

But that was Lydia. She could dare to be different and lived as the woman God created her to be, irrespective of what was at stake.

Lydia's decision to maintain her belief in God after she left Thyatira and was living in Philippi would have looked absurd to people at the time. Much like today, when people who identify with God and serious religion of any nature, can be seen as dense in the head and probably living in an age that is past, gone and forgotten.

Roman Philippi had no room for the worship of the God of Israel. And the character of Philippian citizens, as described previously would be less tolerant to Jewish religious beliefs.

Moreover, social lifestyle of the time was linked to religious life. To the extent that even foods served at social gatherings like harvest feasts, weddings and family gatherings would be made with the remains of foodstuff sacrificed first to pagan deities.

Religious sexual rituals involving multiple intimate partners were part of the celebrations and many practices that were in conflict with the demands of the lifestyle required of adherents of the Jewish God.

Therefore it was likely that Lydia stayed away from activities that would compromise her faith in God. Isolation from these societal norms could cost her a lot. She could lose face in society and business as an immigrant woman.

It could be that the reference of her as *a native of Thyatira* was a derogatory term to describe her anti-social tendencies but was rendered positive by the author of the book of Acts.

Lydia zealously met with women who held similar beliefs as herself. These women would be from different backgrounds but this was irrelevant to her. What was important to Lydia was the fact that, they were willing to worship God with her in the face of potential mockery and threats.

Whatever the situation was, Lydia courageously exhibited autonomy as a minority woman who feared God and stood up for what she believed in without compromise.

Lydia's attitude was a strength that showed what women can do anywhere in the world when they fear God.

The irony though was that unknown to Lydia, God had a plan for her beyond her wildest dreams. To elevate Lydia to be a beacon in the spread of the new religion, Christianity, the offshoot of Judaism, in the European world.

As the story unfolds, it becomes clear that God wants to use her to reach Europe with the Christian faith.

Reflect on these:

1. Do you believe in God?

2. If you do not, do you desire to know about Him?

3. If you do, how do you manage to keep faith in Him in the face of unbelief?

*There is neither Jew nor Greek, slave nor free, male nor
female,
for you are all one in Christ Jesus.*

Galatians 3:28

CHAPTER THREE

GOD HONOURED LYDIA

When it was time for the gospel of Christ to go to Europe, God decided to make a difference in the way that it had been presented to people outside Palestine.

The regular conduit had been preaching the gospel first to Jews. In Philippi however, God decided to reward those who diligently sought Him (Heb. 11:6b). He chose Lydia to be the main contact for Christianity in Europe.

The story unfolds in how the apostle Paul preached the gospel to Lydia and her friends at Philippi.

Paul had ministered in Asia Minor and had established some churches. And so he decided to move next to the most logical places near where he had planted churches. But God had other plans for him so He diverted him to Europe.

I am sure that a gentile woman like Lydia and her friends as founding members of a church was definitely not Paul's idea of ministry.

But when God is in control, His idea rules.

God, Lydia and Paul

Lydia's story occurred in the background of God's choice of Paul as the apostle to the gentiles.

After Jesus Christ died, the twelve disciples concerned themselves mostly with preaching the gospel to Jews in

Palestine and the surrounding regions. Paul who converted later into Christianity became the main bearer of the gospel to the gentiles. It was during one of his evangelistic trips that he came into contact with Lydia.

Paul had done some evangelistic work in Cyprus, Galatia and Phrygia (Acts 13) and decided to minister in the neighbouring regions of Mysia and Bithynia.

Mysia was the north-western part of the province of Asia in the region now known as Turkey. Bithynia was in the eastern part of Mysia. Logically, after Paul evangelized the southern territories which were Galatia and Phrygia, his next move should have been to the upper territories. But the Bible says the Holy Spirit stopped him. The Bible does not state how the Holy Spirit prevented Paul and his friends (the missionaries), but there are several ways that the Holy Spirit could make His will known to believers.

The Holy Spirit could prevent through normal situations like; refusal of entry permits, lack of initial contact (a person, or group), sickness, or lack of money. He could also prevent through spiritual means like; a prophecy, dream, or vision. Either way, He made His will known to the missionaries, so they stopped their work and remained in the city of Troas.

Whiles in Troas, Paul had a vision of a man calling him to come to the European region of Macedonia and help (Acts 16:9). This vision was to become the *"Macedonian Call"* to many Bible students. Paul responded to the vision and the missionaries, traveled to the city of Philippi in Macedonia to preach the gospel of Christ.

But there was a problem!

Paul and his friends could not start work right away. They had to wait!

The waiting

And we stayed there several days. **Acts 16:12b**

Whenever I come across this closing remark in Acts chapter 16 in my studies, it puzzles me and I wonder what the plan of God entails.

The scripture simply said that Paul and his team stayed (same as waited) several days before they started work. No reason was given for this waiting.

Why did they have to stay several days in Philippi before preaching the gospel?

After all, Paul and his friends were stopped from preaching the gospel in Asia. And God through a vision led them to Philippi. You would think that God would make Philippi ready for the gospel when they arrived, but that was not the case.

Again, this was another first time for Paul since he started work as a missionary: waiting in a potential preaching place.

Generally, *waiting on God* would involve pausing from activity and remaining focused on God for direction. *Waiting* is one of the many disciplines of walking with God. Entering into marriage, starting a new job, relocation to a new place and especially starting a Christian ministry would be times that call for this discipline.

Waiting on God might stretch to long periods of time. They could also be just a short time depending on the issues at stake. No specific times would normally be set for *waiting on God*.

Waiting on God would involve a time of prayer, reading and studying the Bible. Sometimes fasting and meditating on the word of God. This special time with God could be approached differently, depending on what works best for each person.

The idea of *waiting* was to spend time with God and receive from Him.

Something we must learn as Christians from this story is the fact that when God show us something to do, we shouldn't assume that because He has given us a vision, everything will go smoothly. As in the case of the missionaries, the reality of the *Macedonian call* was far from just moving to Philippi.

God who gave the vision must also provide direction for what He sanctioned. And one way for us to be sure of His direction is by *waiting* on Him.

In Philippi, Paul and his team went through the rigours of *waiting* as they sought God's direction for ministry in the city.

Three reasons for the waiting

Reason One - New Field

Europe was an entirely new field to the mostly Jewish missionaries. At that time, Europe was a great piece of land filled with peoples of diverse cultures and religious beliefs. Historians described them as barbarians and primitive people.

Their religious beliefs differed from Judaism, from which Christianity stemmed. These Europeans believed in many gods compared to the Jewish/Christian belief in one God.

Romans who were supposed to be the civilised rulers of the time, absorbed many deities from people they had conquered into their own religious life and worshipped many gods. For example, Zeus, the Greek god was the same as the Roman god Jupiter. And Dionysius was Bacchus. And the goddesses, Isis from Egypt and Cybele from Anatolia (Turkey) were all part of Roman pantheon of goddesses.

Even Caesar, the Roman emperor claimed to be god and those who refused to acknowledge him as a god—mostly Jews and Christians—were persecuted. Some were thrown alive to lions to be eaten or burnt at the stake.

Apart from the religious situation, the Philippian citizens' imitation of the sophisticated Roman lifestyle was entirely different from the simple Palestinian Jewish lifestyle that the missionaries knew. Rome ruled Palestine, but Roman culture did not dominate Jewish lifestyle as it did in Philippi.

Rampant display of *Roman lifestyle* in Philippi obviously disgusted these simple Jewish Christians who might have wondered why God chose Philippi as the first place to hear the gospel in Europe.

Paul possibly thought about a change of plan or change of venue. And in his dilemma resorted to retreat from preaching. But the retreat led him to the source for direction, which was God.

Reason Two - No Synagogue

The city of Philippi lacked a significant Jewish community to provide a meeting place—a synagogue—which could be a spring-board for preaching about Christ.

Synagogues were and (are) Jewish meeting places for worship and other social activities. As the Jewish custom required, there can only be a synagogue in a place where a quorum of at least ten Jewish men were found.

When the Bible described Lydia and the women as meeting by the riverside to worship the Jewish God, it implied that the city had no Jewish synagogue. Even though there were people interested in the Jewish religion, there were not enough Jewish men living in Philippi to start a synagogue.

Without a synagogue for Jewish worship, adherents to Judaism could only pray elsewhere. Women could not form a quorum for a synagogue.

Paul had no choice but to wait. It was a major change from the usual way he preached the gospel. Paul always contacted Jews first and went to gentiles only when he was rejected by the Jews (Acts 13:5, 14; 14:1). The book of Acts—especially in chapter 13—records that Paul and Barnabbas preached the gospel in several Jewish synagogues. It was an evangelistic strategy that relied on the *known* to the *unknown*. And followed what the master, Jesus Christ, Himself taught the disciples in **Acts 1:8:**

*But you will receive power when the Holy Spirit come
on you; and
You will be my witnesses in Jerusalem, and in all Judea
and Samaria,
and to the ends of the earth.*

Jesus' teaching followed the progression; to preach the gospel first to the inhabitants of Jerusalem, all Judea, and Samaria and to the end of the world.

There was great wisdom in the order the Lord Jesus Christ gave. The universal logic in *hooking up* first with people from our native backgrounds when in a new place is entrenched in various levels of life.

I remember when I was a new comer to London, UK, and barely knew the place. I was out walking through Nottingham one day, when I heard people speaking my mother tongue. I stopped instantly, approached them and began to ask them where they live, how long they have been in UK, what they do and how to get around.

Having made acquaintance in no time, we exchanged telephone numbers and addresses. They showed me where to shop for traditional foodstuffs in London, where to find local churches and low income housing. It made life easier for me in U.K.

It helps to start from the known to the unknown.

Reason Three-A Woman Contact

At Philippi, God intended to use a woman—Lydia—to be Paul's main contact in preaching the gospel in Europe. This last reason is the most significant to the story of Lydia as portrayed in this book.

In Philippi when the absence of Jews was so evident, Paul's state of mind could be imagined when he was faced with the only option of working with women.

If you consider the social order of the time when women had little to do with religious leadership, and the cultural context of the missionaries which relegated women into the background, this plan of God was real breaking news. In today's rendition, you can imagine major networks like CNN blaring it over the airwaves as something unparalleled!

But it was a big catastrophe for the missionaries. Because for these Jewish men, that was not the religiously right way to do things.

In my opinion, these were the reasons why God led them to wait on Him before they started work.

Effects of the waiting

God taught Paul that He is not a stereotype God who is limited to just one way of doing things.

I am sure Paul saw the proposition of working first with women as a joke. The idea was a challenge in itself, let alone the fact that they were gentile women. Gentiles were barely the right kind of people for Jewish males to interact with.

Paul was a Pharisee, who was zealous for the things of God. Pharisees were said to pray daily thanking God for not making them women.

It would therefore be difficult for him to acknowledge the will of God in the woman Lydia, without divine intervention. Had he not waited, he would have still approached God's work with his own strength and evangelistic know how but overlooked the woman God had chosen to help with the work.

Approaching God's work with our own strength and know how is not always the only way to do Christian things. Sadly, this often happens to even so called seasoned Christians who may choose to use the same methods they know in each case for God's work.

We must always remember that our God is not restricted to one method.

God's choice of Lydia unveiled

The missionaries possibly thought that if they acknowledged the women in Philippi, the first church in Europe would be dominated by women. And a woman would be the church leader when they had to leave town. But they forgot that Christ had made all things new including religious leaders.

When the spiritual exercise of waiting on God released them from these thoughts, they were able to see the unveiled plan of God in which women played major roles.

Lydia and the women the missionaries eventually met at the Philippian riverside were possibly not Jewish. They probably were gentile women who were attracted to the Jewish religion. But they obviously loved the Jewish God to the extent that without the required number of Jewish men to organize a synagogue they still went on worshipping God.

When that realisation dawned on the missionaries they could not help but embrace the all-encompassing greatness of God and let His will be done.

I am not surprised that God chose them as the pinnacle for the European mission. For God delights in those who diligently seek Him at any place, and anywhere in the world.

God does not care for politics, and the culture of patriarchy means nothing to him. He will use women who are committed to him to effect change in society irrespective of the political situation.

In the dark corner of the world at that time in history, God overlooked the status quo and accomplished His purpose with women.

God still looks for devout women who will stand up for him in their own right as human beings created in His image.

Reflect on these:

1. How do you honour the word of God in the light of cultural and societal constraints?

2. Have you ever waited on God as described in the book?

3. Try waiting on God on regular basis as a spiritual discipline. You can start this week.

For we are God's fellow workers; you are God's field, God's building.

I Corinthians 3:9

CHAPTER FOUR

LYDIA, MODEL FOR ALL WOMEN

I don't have the right words to describe my joy, at the discovery that, God's choice of Lydia might have been the main reason why Paul hesitated to start work in Philippi.

From experience, I know how women are discriminated against in religious circles. How women have to cope with hypocritical expressions of male leaders under the guise of religious expression and wrongful interpretations of scripture.

I was not surprised at all that a whole divinely sanctioned project like the *Macedonian call* given to the missionaries in a vision could come to a halt, because a woman was to be involved in its founding stages. As I continued with my studies of Lydia in the book of Acts chapter 16, I simply thanked God for opening my eyes to this truth.

In God's wisdom, He decided to break through the cultural and religious order. And teach the lesson that He loves all human beings and He loves working with women too.

I think Paul's move to accept the Philippian challenge, and his ministry with Lydia and her women, cemented that fact and ushered in, the new status of women in the Christian church.

After the experience of God's choice of Lydia, Paul, was able to evangelise with women including Priscilla and Phoebe, whom he referred to as fellow workers in Christ Jesus (Romans 16: 1-3) without apprehension.

This book will not be complete, without this chapter. A chapter that I have dedicated to the discussion of the relationship between God's choice of Lydia for European Christianization and God's approval of women in Christian ministry in general.

Misunderstandings of parts of scripture have led to situations that prevent women from forefront ministries in many churches. I want us to look at some of these.

Misunderstandings: women and leadership

Relegating women into the background may be shaped by societal and cultural views which discriminate against women but manage to find expression in practical Christianity.

Several well meaning Christians (*whatever that means),* find it difficult to accept God's choice of women in church leadership. But the Bible is clear that women have a place in the Christian ministry.

We women need to understand our place in the church. And begin to appreciate who we are in Christ and not look down on ourselves or any other woman that God wants to use. We should not encourage men to look down at us, as if we are not capable.

Moreover, we should be careful not to follow wrong teachings about our place in the Christian church because God included women in the general plan of Christianity. It is a truth that *knowledge is power.* Therefore, it is only when we have knowledge of our place and worth in the church that we can assume it responsibly.

Even in secular fields, the status of women has changed significantly from what it used to be. Women's role in education, business and family life, support how men and women are increasingly learning to live as equal human beings created in the image of God.

Whereas, some Christian institutions have embraced these changes freely, others continue to struggle and strongly oppose giving women chances in church leadership. Those who oppose often quote scriptures, mostly written by Paul, to support their point like this one:

> *As in the congregations of the saints, women should remain silent in*
> *the churches. They are not allowed to speak, but must be in submission, as*
> *the Law says. If they want to inquire about something, they should ask*
> *their own husbands at home; for it is disgraceful for a woman to speak*
> *in the church.* **1Corinthians 14:33b-35**

My question is, if this scripture is to be interpreted literally, what do women without husbands do if they do not understand anything in the church? Another quotation from the letter Paul wrote to Timothy is a favourite of these Christians:

> *A woman should learn in quietness and full of submission. I do not permit*
> *a woman to teach or to have authority over a man; she must be silent. For*
> *Adam was formed first then Eve. And Adam was not the one deceived; it was*
> *the woman who was deceived and became a sinner. But women will be saved through childbearing - if they continue in faith, love and holiness with*
> *propriety.* **I Timothy 2:11**

Literally interpreted, not all mankind has sinned but only women. Barren women will also never be saved because they have no means for salvation through childbearing.

What these Christians forget is that Paul also argued strongly that:

All have sinned and have come short of the glory of God, and are justified freely by His grace through the redemption that came by Christ Jesus. **Romans 3:23-24**

This quotation makes all mankind sinful and in need of salvation through Jesus Christ by the grace of God. Thus it is not only the woman who is sinful.

There are other Bible verses which support the fact that women can be used in the forefront of God's kingdom business.

Understanding Paul's teachings

If we situate those Bible verses we just read in the right context, we will be able to understand Paul and why he gave those instructions to those women in particular. I believe Paul's concern for the attitude of women in the gentile churches, especially in the church of Corinth, was because of their behaviour. These women were converts from licentious pagan religions and depraved social lifestyles. As mentioned earlier, the pagan religious practices in Europe were unacceptable to Christianity.

Furthermore, these converts essentially, had limited knowledge of the high moral standards required by the Jewish/Christian God. In the Jewish/Christian congregations in Jerusalem and the surrounding areas, similar instructions were not given to women. This is because Jewish-Christian women of the time culturally knew and accepted their place religiously, even though they were liberated in Christ. They were used to the culture of women not being in the forefront in religious affairs, and this cultural stance was conveniently transferred into the Christian church.

The same principle can be likened to Paul's argument of not willing to have gentile believers circumcised. He circumcised Timothy (Acts 16:3) because he had a Jewish mother and the Jews would criticize him, but did not circumcise Titus who was Greek (Galatians 2:3).

Not all the gentile churches received such instruction from Paul regarding women.

It is obvious that those Christian women Paul wrote about were getting out of hand and needed discipline and order. Putting a passage in the cultural and historical context helps to understand what the word of God means at every given time. It will then facilitate proper application of scripture for all times.

The misunderstandings stem from interpreting scripture in a narrow way to suit our own purposes. That is when we interpret scripture out of context.

Bible study must be contextual

It is important to always read a Bible verse within the context it appears. The Bible was written for people who lived at a certain time in history with their own cultures and customs. Therefore, to understand what a verse is about, the reader must consider what is being said in terms of the times; the culture, the audience, the writer and even the reason for the writing.

The languages used for writing the Bible also add meaning to certain verses. The Koine Greek language that was mostly used for writing the New Testament was very rich linguistically. For example, four different Greek words translate into just one English word for *love*. Sometimes, this makes it difficult to get the actual meaning implied by the original writer in the English rendition. This is one of the reasons why we have many different English versions of the Bible.

It is also important to read Bible passages as a whole; paying attention to verses that comes before and after. If we abide by these principles in our approach to studying the Bible, we will understand why certain parts of scripture are written in harsher tones than others. And we will know that God's plan of saving the world includes using women.

God's plan for women

I want to encourage Christian women to avail themselves of opportunities to be used by God in any way He chooses. One powerful scripture written by Paul reveals that the plan of God to the church at large includes women in leadership. God gives ministry gifts equally to members of the church according to these verses:

> *It was He (Christ Himself, emphasis mine) who gave some to be apostles, some prophets, some evangelists and some pastors and teachers, for the equipping of the saints for the work of the ministry, for the edifying of the body of Christ.* **Ephesians 4:11-12**

Paul is speaking to the whole church which includes women. He referred to Christ equipping the church with ministry gifts for both genders for the edification of the church. God who is no respecter of persons does not discriminate between men and women when he blesses the church with gifts.

God used many women in forefront ministries in the Bible, even when there were men around. For example, God used Huldah, the prophetess to interpret and validate the book of the Law, found in the temple during the reign of King Josiah. Huldah was a prophetess, a contemporary of the prophet Habakkuk. Even though we have the prophet Habakkuk's book in the Bible, he was passed by when the King needed a Prophet to interpret the word of God. The High Priest Hilkiah, preferred to go to Huldah, a woman (2Kings 22:11-20).

Deborah the prophetess was another key figure in Israelite political administration (Judges 4: 4-5). I will later explore her distinct qualities in the section that will look at Lydia as a Christian working woman. God used these women even in those very patriarchal times of the Old Testament.

Yes, they are isolated cases, but don't forget that Bible writers like Paul, lived in times that were very patriarchal, and their writings focused on the great works of "men" not women. But God still allows us glimpses of women He used.

It is no wonder that God re-echoed what He had done before in the choice of Lydia to straighten His plan for world evangelization. God still uses women and will continue until the end of age.

The LORD Jesus Christ respected women

In the New Testament, Christ showed respect for women during his ministry on earth. He listened to women, allowed them to sit together with men as he preached and did not burden them with segregation and inferiority. There is nowhere in the New Testament accounts about Jesus that He looked down on the female gender.

Of course, Jesus did not choose a woman among His twelve disciples, but it is important to understand the culture in which he started his ministry. Christianity was built on the Jewish religion and culture, so the twelve disciples were in a sense a cultural representation of the twelve tribes of Israel.

Mary Magdalene, Joanna, the wife of Cuza, Susanna and others were devout women who were part of Jesus' traveling team (Luke 8:1-3).

Jesus Christ put value on womanhood and showed their place in the gospel ministry by entrusting them with important messages. He revealed the good news to the Samaritan woman whose description makes her a great sinner (John 4:17-18). Even before his messianic mystery was made clear to his male disciples, he chose to reveal it to this non-Jewish Samaritan woman who listened to him. This woman went out and told others about Christ and the Bible says:

Many of the Samaritans from the town believed in Him because of the woman's testimony. **John 4:39**

Why would Christ even before commissioning his disciples to preach the gospel to the world, choose a gentile woman to be his evangelist if he did not want women actively involved in ministry?

He also revealed the awesome mystery of his resurrection to Mary Magdalene and other women while the male apostles were hiding (John 20:1-18). Christ never said; "these are women so I would not let them bear the good news."

By these examples, the Lord Jesus Christ is telling us that following Him means changing the cultural order and ushering in a new one. In this new order, all mankind will respect and help each other to reach their God-given potentials.

Hence, in the economy of God, a woman who has been created in the image of God is considered the same as a man. She can be used equally as man if it is in the will and plan of God.

That is why God chose the woman Lydia in Philippi and opened her heart to understand and receive the gospel.

Reflect on these:

1. Do you feel comfortable that God wants to use you as a woman in the Church?

2. List some ways that you think God can use you in your family, neighbourhood, workplace and in the church as a woman?

3. Pray about this list and ask God to open doors for you to serve Him.

As for me and my household, we will serve the Lord.

Joshua 24:15b

CHAPTER FIVE

LYDIA AND HER HOUSEHOLD ACCEPTED CHRIST

Lydia knew and worshipped God but when she came into contact with Paul she became saved into eternal life by listening to the good news about Jesus Christ. When Lydia believed in the Christian faith, her whole household also believed.

It is not easy today for a household to boast that all its members believe in God as people know and have a right to choose what they want to believe in. In the New Testament times, people from different parts of the world believed in different gods.

Lydia's household members wouldn't be different. Even if they were slaves or just employees in her service, they had some right to their beliefs. However, the Bible says that Lydia, and her household responded to the gospel and converted to the Christian faith.

I believe Lydia's household members did not all convert at once, even though that could be possible. Whichever way it happened, Lydia contributed to lead them to Christ. My point here is that, family heads have a responsibility to the spiritual development of their family members.

In the case of Lydia, it began first with her.

Lydia met Paul

Lydia first met Paul in Philippi at a riverside where she was busily worshipping God with other women on their regular Sabbath day worship. Most likely, this was their regular routine. There is a Bible verse in **Hebrews 10:25** that admonish that:

Let us not give up meeting together, as some are in the habit of doing,
but let us encourage one another – and all the more as you see the
Day approaching.

Lydia and the women were limited in their knowledge about God but they remained constant in worshiping Him. Imagine them praying fervently for God to send enough Jewish men to Philippi so that they could build a synagogue. And God, who had something better for them than just a synagogue, heard their prayers. In His own time, He sent the missionaries with the gospel that would bring them full salvation.

Interestingly, a man beckoned Paul to come to Macedonia in the vision, but in reality, a woman—Lydia—and her women friends prayed and readied themselves for the gospel. This is one of the situations I like to explain as a cultural paradigm.

It was possible that Paul would eagerly respond to a vision that showed a man in need more than a woman. Furthermore, a man in a vision was more culturally presentable to Paul as he relayed the vision to the other missionaries than a woman. God might have therefore decided to use this medium of communication in that situational context to appeal to Paul and the missionaries. Of course, this is just a speculation, but a safe one to help us understand the context of the Lydia story. The bottom line was that, God used that cultural means of communication to bait Paul to Philippi where he was needed most.

After Paul finally decided to share the gospel in Philippi he found the devout women who were thirsty for the things of God. Imagine Lydia and her friends' joy when they met the Jewish men. And the surprise of the missionaries when the *Macedonian call* unveiled in the form of Lydia and her women friends.

Lydia met Paul there for the first time.

Lydia accepted Christ

Lydia had zeal in the things of God but was limited in the knowledge of the saving grace of the Lord Jesus Christ. She knew virtually nothing about the gospel of Jesus Christ.

The gospel is simply Christ crucified for the sins of mankind. It offers salvation from eternal destruction through the forgiveness of sins. The gospel also offer benefits including everlasting life to all those who will accept the Lord Jesus Christ as their personal saviour (John 3:16).

In addition to accepting Christ, people build a personal relationship with God as their father (John 1:12) and live in the assurance that they are the children of God saved by the His grace. Lydia's searching heart was poised for a message like this.

Lydia could be likened to many people who grew up in religious homes, have had several religious experiences, and feel automatically qualified as Christians, because they attend church, are generous and observe Christian holidays like lent, Christmas, Good Friday and have Christian parents.

But there is no automatic Christian.

Assertions like *I was born into the church* and *my parents were Christians* do not make a person a Christian. People must be Christians in their own rights. Just as the Lord Jesus Christ told the religious leader, Nicodemus, that:

> *I tell you the truth; no one can see the kingdom of God unless he is born again.* **John 3:3**

Now this term *born again* has become a common expression in many Christian circles to describe the experience of converting into the Christian faith. Lydia had a similar experience after years of religiously worshipping the One True God.

To be born again simply means to make a decision to accept the Lord Jesus Christ as a personal saviour. It is only then that you can confidently say that *you are a born again Christian.*

Lydia did that when God opened her heart to understand Paul's preaching of the gospel. She first made a personal decision to be *born again* in Christ. And literally asked the Lord Jesus Christ to come into her life and be her Lord and saviour.

Salvation is a free gift from God, but people must accept it to make it theirs. Without accepting this free gift, salvation will ever remain a wrapped gift, beautifully tied up in ribbons where people do not make the move to unwrap and take possession.

I did it once in my teenage years when I listened to a preacher talk about the saving grace of the Lord Jesus Christ.

I want to devote this part to briefly present to you how you can accept the everlasting gift of Christ in case you have not had the opportunity to personally invite the Lord Jesus Christ into your life. This is how it is done:

The Bible in **Romans 3:23** says that:

For all have sinned and fall short of the glory of God.

And in **Romans 10:9-10,** the scripture says that:

That if you confess with your mouth, "Jesus is Lord," and believe in your heart that
God raised him from the dead, you will be saved. For it is with your heart that you
believe and are justified, and it is with your mouth that you confess and are saved.

So the process begins when people:

a. **Acknowledge** their sinful nature as descendants of Adam (The Bible teaches that since the sin of the first man—Adam—all mankind have sinned and as a result have come short of the glory of God. When Adam and Eve disobeyed God and ate the fruit in the Garden of Eden, men lost good relationship they had with God. And throughout the generations men had tried to make right their relationship with God through several means including observing religious rituals. But they are all to no avail, until God provided a means through Jesus Christ. That is why it is only through Jesus Christ that a person can be right with God.)

Jesus said:

I am the way and the truth and the life. No one comes to the Father except through me. **John 14:6**

b. **Believe in** the saving grace of the Lord Jesus Christ. (God provided Jesus Christ as a means to bridge the gap between Him and mankind. Now because Christ died for the sinful man, it is possible for us sinful men to have a right relationship with God through Jesus Christ.)

c. **Confess** their sins and accept Christ as a personal saviour by inviting him into their lives. (Salvation is a free gift offered by God but until we accept it, it remains a gift.)

You can invite Christ now into your life by simply asking Him in with your own words. Or you can use this sample prayer below:

Dear Lord Jesus, I believe that I am a sinner and
cannot make myself right with God. I accept the gift of
salvation through thy grace. I believe you died for me.
And I invite you into my life to be my Lord and Saviour.
Hence forth, I ask that my life will be controlled by your
Holy Spirit and that I will live the rest of my life for you.
Thank you for answered prayer. Amen.

Lydia would have been filled with joy and hope in her new faith in Jesus Christ. Just like others before her in the Bible (Acts: 42-47). And most of us who did this sometime in our lives.

Afterwards, she desired that all the people close to her would share in her new experience.

Lydia's household converted

Once Lydia accepted God's gift of salvation, she knew it was too valuable to keep it to herself. She ensured that her household members heard the gospel for themselves. It is likely that she attended the riverside prayer meetings with them or some of them.

On the other hand, a thoughtful woman like Lydia might have envisaged how difficult it would be, for her as a Christian to live with people who do not believe in Christ. As many believers in Christ attest to this, especially those Christians whose spouses do not believe in Christ. They tell of how they suffer in an attempt to follow their faith.

Lydia prayed and created the opportunity for the members of her household to hear the gospel. When at last they understood the gospel for themselves, they all invited Christ into their lives and experienced the new life in Christ Jesus.

The fact is; we don't have to force people to accept Christ, but we can influence them by several means. And one of these means is when Christian parents assume the role of educating their children in the things of God. That is the next thing I will discuss.

Christian education must begin at home

Most education including Christian education is done in regular and Sunday Schools. But I strongly believe that Christian education should begin at home and not be limited to Sunday School Teachers who only have Sunday mornings at their disposal. It is more important today, when religion is not part of the regular school's curriculum.

When I was growing up, the school day started with a prayer and a Christian Hymn. We read the Bible afterwards and in fact Bible Knowledge (B.K.) was a compulsory subject in the academic curriculum, irrespective of a pupil's religious background. Basic morals like love, tolerance, honesty and kindness were taught in B.K. class.

It is not the same today. In its place several academic topics are taught and sometimes religious classes even turn out to be the worse place for religious education. For the Christian parent, there is no excuse but to find a time to teach your children your religious beliefs.

The Bible is a good source for both the religious and moral instruction. It offers a whole range of topics. Several Bible versions have pages at the beginning or end of the main Bible books, with topics and their references. For example; under the topic *love*, there will be lists of Bible passages that talks about love. Each verse will give an idea of how to apply the abstract concept of *love* in everyday life. The same applies to questions on parenting, finances, time, life plans, career, marriage and even sex before marriage. These are all life issues that come up at a point in the lives of family members and parents can discuss in an educational session with their children.

As parents understand their role and responsibility to educate family members, and zealously work at it, they will help shape society for the better. The Bible says that:

Train a child the way he should go, and when he is old he will not depart from it. **Proverbs 22:6**

I spoke to several Christian grandparents who raised their children with the Bible. Majority of them said that their children are active in the Lord and are raising their own children with the Bible just as they (the grandparents) did.

We parents must know that our responsibilities to our children exceed providing food, shelter and clothing. And this includes providing spiritual, emotional and psychological support to our children. We must always remember that we will be accountable to God for our parenting, so we better watch out how we do it.

Lydia gave her household the best gift any caregiver could give. She gave them the opportunity to know Christ in a personal way.

Daily Family Devotion

One of the ways to do Christian education in a family setting is when the family comes together to do what is called family devotion. It is a time in the day that a family can manage to get all the members in the household at a sitting for a religious discussion.

I lived with a Christian family for some time in my life and one of the things I learnt from them was how the family came together each morning to do devotion.

It was a time of prayer and Bible reading. Even the youngest member of the family was encouraged to share something during the Bible discussions. During the prayer time, the leader who was usually the father or the mother would ask family members for prayer topics and we would pray about them as a family. We also shared our experiences of the day and traded ideas with one another.

I have included this in my bank of parenting in my own family and I find it very beneficial. Sometimes we are not able to do it in the morning but in the night before we go to bed.

Reading the Bible and praying as a family is a good way to stay together. Devotions furthermore provide the forum to get closer to each other. People may have needs to be prayed for and also blessings to thank God for. The whole family in this way affirm the sovereignty of God over their lives.

There a lot of materials in bookshops and on the internet for family devotions. Usually devotional books or cards have specific Bible passages for each day throughout the year. Some families just read the Bible books chapter by chapter. We must be wise and choose what works for our families. What is important is that we make sure that we maintain a daily routine of family devotion.

Reflect on these:

1. Do you know Christ in a personal way as your Saviour? If not take time to think about it.

2. What about your family members? Is there someone who doesn't know Christ?

3. This week share Christ with a family member.

PART TWO

LYDIA - HER DISTINCT QUALITIES

She sets about her work vigorously; her arms are strong for her tasks
She sees that her trading is profitable, and her lamp does not go out at night.

Proverbs 31:17-18

CHAPTER SIX

LYDIA, AN INDUSTRIOUS WOMAN

This chapter begins part two of this book. Lydia's story moves to a section which presents her distinct qualities as implied by the biblical narrative.

As part of her distinct qualities, Lydia was an industrious woman. She had a career in business as a seller of purple cloth. In those days, women mostly took charge of the home. And Lydia had a home to manage, but she also knew that there was need for her to engage in business outside her home to be able to provide financial support for her family.

She worked.

In the book of Proverbs chapter 31 verses 10 to 31, the daily routine of a nameless biblical woman with an equal sense of industry best described Lydia. The passage originally described a married woman but it could also apply to any hard-working married or unmarried woman. As this industrious woman kept her household in good state, she also managed business outside home, and even invested in real estate. The quotation at the beginning of this chapter best described her day to day business activity.

Like this industrious woman in Proverbs, Lydia mastered her domestic and public worlds, and excelled in delivering both duties.

How Lydia did it is what this chapter presents.

Lydia sold purple cloth

In the Bible story Lydia was described in a simple statement as *a native of Thyatira who was a purple cloth dealer*. But those simple words actually described an ancient successful, international, business tycoon.

Purple colour in those days was a symbol of royalty. The Caesars and the upper class in the Roman Empire wore purple cloth. It was called *the color of the emperor*. Obviously, Lydia dealt with this upper crust: the rich and influential people in the Roman Empire.

Historians talked about the prosperous purple trade in the Roman world in different categories. Different types of the purple dye existed in many parts of the empire including the most popular dye which was invented in Tyre, known as *the Tyrian Dye*. Extracted from the glands of a shell fish, this expensive dye produced a brilliant, rich, crimson shade of purple that became the royal favourite.

In Lydia's hometown Thyatira, a similar industry was booming. But instead of the dye being extracted from the shell fish, the Thyatirians extracted from the root of a plant called *madder* which produced a lesser quality and was considered as one of the cheapest dyes available. However, the different types of purple on the market met the needs of all classes of *nobility*. Archaeologists have excavated inscriptions relating to the guild of Purple Dyers in the ruins of Thyatira, the hometown of Lydia. These guilds were exclusive trade unions that protected the rights of its members.

Lydia was living in Philippi and most likely involved in this intercontinental export/import business. As a textile merchant, she possibly owned companies that dyed purple fabrics, designed a line of clothing and retailed in a chain of shops in Asia and Europe. She might have imported from Asia, either the expensive purple cloth from Tyre or the imitation product from her native Thyatira. Most probably, Lydia dealt in both products including other types of purple clothes that were on the market at the time like any smart business woman.

As Lydia stocked her warehouse with different types of purple clothes, she offered a wide range of choices to her customers. Her target of course would be doing business with royalty but then, society always have the new rich and the middle class, all trying to climb the social ladder. And in those days, there was no better way for people to communicate their place in society than what they wore.

Clothing has always been a means of communication. In some communities wearing black signifies bereavement and white victory. A man in a white toga with purple borders for instance in the Roman world belonged to the senate which was the ruling class.

Lydia focused on meeting the needs of the people she served in business.

Lydia Excelled in her business

Lydia did not just sell purple cloth; she excelled in the sales. She was in an exclusive business for textile merchants who were able to deal with people of the upper class. Maintaining these high net-worth clients was not easy; these were people who could easily get better services from other sources. It was not clear how Lydia did it, but it's likely that she learned business administration, put her customers' interest first, diversified products in her shop and possibly controlled the market.

One thing about successful people is that they usually go beyond the regular requirements of their professions and add on their own unique style. That piece they add on distinguishes them and set them apart from all others. In contemporary times, this is often seen as *models of distinction* which in actual fact are the individuals' own *distinctiveness*.

An example was a smart businessman who introduced the concept of reducing goods by one cent with the .99cents at the end of prices in a time when the concept was foreign in his community. Even though the same products flooded the market, customers bypassed them to go to his shop for the reduced one cent without considering the amount of time and money they spent to get to his shop. This businessman made a lot of profit within a short time.

Lydia worked hard to excel. Successful women work day and night to accomplish their goals. Excelling in anything; education, career, or even parenting calls for hard work. Successful people of old toiled relentlessly to realize their dreams.

If somebody prophesies to you that God will make you a millionaire and you decide to lie in bed, eat and watch television, it will not happen no matter how strong your faith in God. However, God will bless your efforts, no matter how small they may be to fulfill the prophecy. The saying goes that: *God helps those who help themselves.*

Despite the fact that Lydia's story portrays the success of a God-fearing woman in her work, many Christian women struggle with going to work outside the home. Often because they have been indoctrinated to think that a woman's place is at home especially when the woman happens to be a wife and a mother. But there are biblical examples of women like Lydia who worked and were successful in what they did.

Biblical women who worked

The Bible shows examples of several God-fearing women who worked in both the Old and New Testaments. These women feared God and worked both inside and outside the home to support their families and their communities.

Deborah (Judges Chapter 4) was a Jewish wife, who worked as a judge of Israel in the Old Testament times. She held an executive position like that of a prime minister and was required to properly administer her time and talents to the benefit of her people. In the capacity as a Judge, Deborah listened to complaints and administered justice. She carried both spiritual and social mandates of serving the nation, and she did it effectively. She was so efficient that her military general Barak would not go to battle without her. Barak needed Deborah's company to boost his morale for battle. If Deborah could manage a husband, family and profession as a judge in those patriarchal times what should stand in the way of today's woman who has modern technology at her disposal.

The midwives Shipporah and Puah (Exodus chapter 1:15-21) were professional nurses who took their work seriously. They risked their lives by saving the Hebrew babies and did not obey Pharaoh's orders to kill them. They knew their job well and excelled in practice as health professionals whose first duty was to save lives. The Lord blessed them with courage and wisdom to go on saving lives in the face of Pharaoh's threats. It takes a God-fearing, ambitious woman to be committed to her career amidst threats and mockery.

Jesus neither asked women to stay home and look after children nor limit their career options only to the domestic sphere. His traveling team included women of substance who footed the bills from their own resources (Luke 8:2-3). These women might have had steady sources of income to be able to do so. The New Testament further presents Dorcas (Acts 9:36-42) who was a dressmaker and Priscilla who worked alongside her husband and Paul as a tentmaker (Acts 18:3).

The Bible is not a manual for women and work so the subject of the various jobs women did is not the main theme. Yet these biblical accounts show that Christian women can work inside and outside home and do not negate their involvement in any kind of work. Christian women just have to be wise in their choices. As Lydia exhibited, women have rights to set goals and accomplish them in any career of their choice.

Woman, man's work companion

God's purpose for creating woman was to provide man with a companion who would be his helper (Genesis 2:20-24). Note that God neither provided man with a housemaid nor a servant to meet his domestic needs.

God could have given man a robot as a helpmate to use as he pleases, but God gave him a woman; a companion of equal intelligence, grace and purpose. Hence, if humankind has developed to separate their domestic and public spheres of life, men and women should equally share the burden of managing both spheres.

Consequently, man should express the need for the woman—his helper—beside him at the public sphere of workplace outside home. It is not as if a woman's help is only needed in home management: ironing shirts, raising babies, cooking and meeting man's sexual needs. Do not get me wrong. These are noble duties that wives undertake with joy, but if a woman can do more than that, why should she be restricted?

When Jesus finished the parable about the shrewd steward, which teaches some important life principles, He said:

The master commended the dishonest steward because he had acted shrewdly.
For the people of this world are shrewd in dealing with their own kind than are
the people of the light. **Luke 16: 8**

Jesus was not asking his followers to be dishonest but to be wise and be able to make use of all the resources available to them. Women are natural resource to help men in any venture. And they should be allowed to fulfill that natural mandate as helpmates to men.

Lydia excelled against men at their own game.

It is sad to observe that many women can only make it successfully in their careers through dubious means. Either by exchanging sexual favours with powerful individuals or stepping over others to reach the top. But these should not be the right way to do things. Women should believe in themselves as capable to reach the top through hard work, diligence and perseverance in the fear of God.

An added incentive is for a woman who fears God to continue to pray and ask for God's grace to become what she was created to be. Instead of focusing on what others and the society wants her to be.

Some Christians frown at successful career mothers and label them as inadequate mothers forgetting that, for some women, including many single mothers, the salaries they earn is the only source of income for their entire families.

Work does not kill and working to support one's family should not be shameful. Christian women are not expected to only occupy themselves with religious activities to the neglect of their responsibilities. The reality though, is that Christians need to work to be able to provide financially for their families and God's work.

Unless God wills it so, He would not rain *manna and quails* to idle Christians who can work, but choose not to. The Bible commends hard work and discourages idleness. Even Paul who was considered as one of the greatest evangelist of all times, talked about his secular work alongside the preaching of the gospel (Acts 18:3).

In the past, women mostly worked around the home. Working in public places was not common and many mothers did not have to work. Society then assumed that a mother's place was to be at home; raising children and caring for the domestic needs of the household. But society has changed a lot and things are not the same as they were before. Women can now choose to be mothers and have careers. Daycares, after school programs and other substitute care arrangements exist in several communities that provide support to mothers who want to pursue other things in their lives.

It is not to say that being a mother and a career woman is easy. Mothering is a complete job in itself, so any additional work becomes an extra. I am a working mother myself and I can testify to this. But it is workable, and women who need to work should not be discouraged. After all, Christians believe that *all things are possible with God*. So then, why is it not possible for a Christian woman to work and maintain a family?

If you are a woman who does not consent to mediocrity, then get up and set a career goal for yourself today. From now on, let us work together to realize this goal.

Reflect on these:

1. What do you dream to be in the next five years?

2. Do you have plans of how to get there?

3. Take some time to research and plan.
   - Research on the internet and at the library;
   - Ask people in the same career of your choice about how they did it;
   - Call your Community Centre or support centres for help;

Set your goals now:

Begin with a *concrete vision and a time frame asking yourself questions and answering like the following example:*

Question: **What do I want to be by a certain time?**
Answer: **To own a childcare centre in the next six years.**
This will help you set a **long term** *goal.*

Question: **How do I realise my set goal?**
Answer: **Develop step by step workable plans**
This will help you set a **short term** *goal.*

Example of a detailed plan:

- Research for the program on the internet or talk to people who have done it and contact schools that do the program;

- Decide on a program; that is either a college level course or a university program;

- Check if you need to do prerequisite courses, complete courses needed for a high school diploma for instance;

- Devote a time for preparation, a year for instance to save for tuition or apply for financial aid;

- Fill the application forms, make financial and childcare plans if you have children;

- Prepare yourself psychologically for the change in your lifestyle

- Go for it!

She watches over the affairs of her household.

Proverbs 31:27

CHAPTER SEVEN

LYDIA HEADED A HOUSEHOLD

A t this point, it is clear that Lydia was a single woman and possibly a single mother.

The Bible referred to Lydia as having a household without mentioning a husband. In those times, it would have been inappropriate to imply that a woman was the head of the house if there was a husband.

We are not told what led to Lydia being in charge of a household but just like any single mother, it could be as a result of several reasons.

A small number of single women may choose to be single in their own right and be in charge of households. But the majority do not make that choice. They rather become victims of situations that they have no control over. When a husband dies or leaves a woman and when a woman has a child with a man she is not married to or living with, she automatically becomes the sole parent who has to raise the child.

Some women also become head of households when they assume care of their siblings or relatives due to death, or sickness in the family. Lydia might have been either a widow who inherited the household from a deceased spouse or just a single woman by choice.

As pertaining to households in those days, there would be children, relatives, slaves and employees living in Lydia's house. As such her household members would be of different ages and from diverse cultural backgrounds. Slaves for instance were often people from conquered nations and considered lower class in the society.

Despite the fact that the biblical narrative did not state that Lydia had children of her own, she could have been a mother and so could be considered as a single mother who was in charge of her household.

Lydia would be in charge of both men and women in her house and would be responsible of ensuring the smooth running of her household. The irony was, she managed them very well and efficiently, despite the fact that she was a single woman, and lived at a time when little was expected of women.

Lydia's household

As a typical household headed by a woman, Lydia's situation would not be different from what pertains today. Her household would depend on one income. This sole income provided for all the financial needs of the family, which would include shelter, clothing, food, medical and entertainment.

Beside the financial situation, Lydia would play both roles of mother and father. She was the spiritual leader responsible for moral education and emotional support of the household. As a God fearing woman, Lydia knew what was morally acceptable and obviously handed it down to her household members in an appropriate manner. She executed her duties well that nothing inappropriate was written about her. It would have been difficult in those times considering that a woman had no place at all in educating others. Her ability to meet these responsibilities obviously came from her faith in God, whom she would reach-out to for support in difficult times.

Lydia was in authority, but she did not abuse her power. She possibly delegated responsibilities to members of the household according to their abilities, and positively supported them to make good choices for their lives. The fruit of that support was evidenced in the choice they made to follow the Christian faith.

Even though Lydia's household was mentioned briefly in the narrative, the impression that was given was that of a healthy and stable family.

Whoever thought that a single woman was not capable of maintaining order and stability in a family, should read the story of Lydia.

Lydia's situation and sexuality

How Lydia handled her sexual needs as a Christian single woman in biblical times is a delicate topic to explore. A topic overlooked and considered as sensitive in Christian circles. Women are human beings with sexual needs and Lydia definitely had them. As the Christian faith is against any form of sexual intimacy outside marriage, when women happen to be single and Christians they act as if they have no urges and suffer in silence. I have yet to hear a Christian church discuss this all important topic. The reality is that whether discussed or not it is real and ever present. Single mothers who may be single not by choice but by circumstances beyond their control are the ones who suffer the most.

Lydia respected God and lived to glorify Him but she was not married and had no man in her life to meet her sexual needs. The Bible neither said that she had a partner nor set apart for the service of God. From the way stories were told about the early Christians, if Lydia had had a secret partner, it would have been documented.

Not long after the story of Lydia's encounter with the missionaries, there was a case regarding sexual immorality between some members of the Church in Corinth which was recorded in I Corinthians chapter 5. The fact that there was no such a thing mentioned or even implied in Lydia's story indicated that she handled herself well. She might have decidedly stayed away from things that would get her in the mood of seeking sexual satisfaction and concentrated on her work and faith in God.

In the church of Corinth Paul admonished the unmarried that it is better to marry than burn with passion (1Corinthians 7:8-9).

A more practical solution to this problem was presented at a recent support group meeting organised for some single mothers. When this issue of sexual needs came up for discussion, it took over the whole meeting. Women with long years of experience as single mothers talked about how frustrating it was to not be able to meet sexual needs because of their choice to be Christians. There were funny but also insightful suggestions.

One mother noted that she tries to focus on her Bible devotions for the day (which obviously talks about the things of God), in order to take her mind off her sexual needs. She emphasised that it's not as if the need does not exist, she simply ignores it by constantly memorizing her Bible reading for the day.

Another single mother said she usually avoid things that would lead her to amorous feelings like watching erotic or *X rated* and *adults only* movies. And refrain from reading sensual books like *Harlequin, Silhouette, Mills and Boons* romances and novels in that genre.

An older single mother added that she found involvement in church activities as not only spiritually benefiting but also helpful in relegating sexual desires to the background. She concluded that her mind would mostly be occupied with her role in the next church activity that she wouldn't have time to think about sex.

One suggestion that all the single mothers seemed to agree on was to network with others to form a support link of people with similar experiences. Interestingly, this was one thing that was very clear in the Lydia narrative in the Bible. She met constantly with other women to pray on the riverside. Most likely, these women might have been in the same situation as herself.

Lydia could have spent her leisure time with unbelieving friends and influential clients in her milieu of high society. She could even have secured a secret partner or toys to meet her sexual needs. But she chose to pray with believing women by the riverside in Philippi. It was possible Lydia reasoned that spending time in the company of business associates whose values differed from hers was not the best thing to do as a Christian. She knew the scriptures and might have read what the Psalmist advised:

> *Blessed is the man who does not walk in the counsel of*
> *the wicked or stand*
> *in way of sinners or sit in the seat of mockers. But his*
> *delight is in the Law of*
> *the Lord, and on his law he meditates day and night.*
> ***Psalm 1:1-2***

However, this is not to say that Christian single women should stay away from social activities and friends who are not Christians. It is to encourage Christian women to make good choices about the people they spend time with.

Make use of every situation

In closing this chapter I want us to look at how best women can make use of every situation they find themselves in especially if they happen to be without partners. Even in worst situations, something good can come out. Being single is not always dis-advantageous. It has its benefits as well.

When women desire to make use of their potential they sometimes need to make decisions that may not favour other people in their lives. Advancing a career or making a major financial decision for instance would be a decision that single women would make easily. Women with partners however, could not simply do that. They would need to think it through with their partners and agree on *something* that will work for them. That *something* may not be what they wanted in the first place, but they will have no choice because in a relationship, sometimes, one must forgo things for others.

As Paul said in 1Corinthians 7:32-35, the responsibilities of married life make it difficult for married people to devote more time to the things of God. And sometimes even to their personal-life developments.

Single women like Lydia make their own decisions. So if you are single today, look at the positive side of things and do something with your life before you settle down and have to think for two.

I am sure; Lydia planned her single life in such a way to make it successful.

For most women, to dream, to wish, to plan, to set goals and aspire to accomplish them are simply inactive, passive, qualities presently dormant in their lives waiting to be rekindled. Let the story of Lydia shake you up to explore your potential if you are still wishing and dreaming. Remember, Lydia was a single woman who became successful in her career as well as managed her household well. She did these at a time when women had virtually no authority in society. And she succeeded even though she had no support from a partner.

Reflect on these:

1. How are you managing your household?

2.   How do you meet your sexual needs? *(Remember that, whatever you do to meet your needs must glorify the Lord).*

3.   How can you benefit from your present situation; married or unmarried to be the woman you dream to be?

When she and the members of her household were baptized, she
invited us to her home. "If you consider me a believer in the Lord,"
she said, "come and stay at my house." And she persuaded us.

Acts 16:15

CHAPTER EIGHT

LYDIA, A HOSPITABLE WOMAN

A book about Lydia cannot end without mention of her act of hospitality. So this chapter is devoted to the subject of Lydia's hospitality to the Christian missionaries.

Actually, the Bible did not use the word hospitality directly in the story of Lydia. Nevertheless, her hosting the missionaries in her home was a classic example of Christian hospitality.

Lydia did not only provide materially to the needs of the missionaries, she helped them spiritually with their ministry of starting a church in Philippi. This church, which most likely began in Lydia's house, became the first Christian church in Europe.

In this chapter there will be a brief discussion on hospitality and Christian hospitality in regards to what Lydia offered the missionaries.

What is hospitality?

Today, hospitality is understood differently by many people and what may be acceptable in one situation may not be the same in another. The following examples explain this point clearly.

A woman went to a book stand to buy a book. When she asked the bookseller for a book on hospitality, a by-stander who was flipping through the pages of a book looked up and asked: "are you taking a course in tourism or hotel industry?"

The bookseller on the other hand remarked, "I have never come across any book on hospitality," looking at the woman with a frown she concluded. "Hospitality is such a normal thing to do without learning about the specifics from a book."

The bookseller and the by-stander understood hospitality from two different perspectives. To the bookseller, it is an everyday kindness that needs no coaching, and to the by-stander it is as a commercialized industry. These views are not different from the views of the general population whose understandings of hospitality are shaded by their cultural undertones.

From an African perspective, hospitality evokes the notion of welcoming nucleus and extended family members. As well as members from one's village, country and strangers to your home without notice for unspecified periods of time. In this context, hospitality becomes a communal responsibility.

In several western cultures however, hospitality could simply mean, having a meal together in a home setting or in a restaurant with friends, neighbours or family. Bed and breakfast accommodation could also be considered as hospitality. Here the concept of hospitality is more individualistic than communal.

These are but some notions of hospitality which makes it more important to situate Christian hospitality as practiced by Lydia.

Lydia's Christian hospitality

To Lydia a believer in God, hospitality was a moral obligation and a command from God. She knew about the scriptures that admonished believers to treat strangers with kindness, love and affection, like this Old Testament verse below where God ordered the people of Israel:

When an alien lives with you in your land, do not mistreat him. The
alien living with you must be treated as one of your

native born. Love
him as yourself, for you were aliens in Egypt. **Leviticus**
19:33-34

This scripture explains hospitality more as showing kindness and love to strangers without expecting anything back.

In addition to this, Lydia might have learnt about Christ's teachings on hospitality including the classic story of the Good Samaritan in Luke 10:25-37. A touching story about a stranger from Samaria (enemy people of the Jews), who kindly helped an injured Jewish man.

As believers are supposed to do, Lydia practiced these teachings of the Bible.

Lydia's Motive and attitude

Lydia had a good motive and a genuine desire to do what Christ would want her to do to strangers. Her words of invitation were:

If you consider me a believer in the Lord, she said,
"come and stay at my house."
Acts 16:15b

Take note that Lydia's invitation was based on the Lord Jesus Christ whom she believed was the Lord of her life. She had no need of favours from the missionaries. After all, she worshipped God before she came into contact with them. Lydia was rich and well situated in the Philippian society. It was not as if inviting the missionaries to her home would boost her popularity in Philippi.

Christianity was not as popular as it is today.

In fact, Christianity at the time was a minority, despised, religious sect that attracted the low-class in society. Lydia by her actions, was rather risking ridicule and mockery to associate with the lowly missionaries.

But Lydia was in a sense showing her gratitude to God and acknowledging His blessings to her. For all that she possessed was a blessing from God. In her act of gratitude, Lydia was living the words of Christ as a good follower whom the Lord would some day remind with the following words that:

> *For I was hungry, and you gave Me nothing to eat, I was thirsty and you gave me nothing to drink, I was a stranger, and you did not invite me in, I needed clothes and you did not clothe me, I was sick and in prison and you did not look after me. They also will answer, 'Lord when did we see you hungry or thirsty or a stranger or needing clothes or sick or in prison, and did not help you?' He will reply, 'I tell you the truth, whatever you did not do for one of the least of these, you did not do for me.'* **Matthew 25:42- 45**

Lydia translated her motive into pleasant attitudes and allowed the missionaries to stay in her home as long as needed.

Have you ever been a guest in a home where you longed for the day you would leave? I have, and it was not a pleasant feeling. But when Lydia invited the missionaries into her house she showed to them that she wanted them to enjoy her hospitality.

Meanwhile, having the right motivation and the right attitude would not rule out unexpected situations. Hence the need to be aware of what hospitality would involve in practical terms. The hospitality Lydia showed the missionaries involved time and money. She also risked her privacy.

Costs involved in hospitality

Money

Paul and his team neither paid for rent nor food when they lived in Lydia's home. From Lydia's business background, the financial cost might have been the least of her worries. But, let us face facts. Feeding a household in addition to four grown-up men for an unlimited period of time would have been a challenge.

Paul's team was at least made up of four men. He began the mission trip with Silas from Syrian Antioch (Acts 15:40). They picked up Timothy from Lystra in Galatia (Acts 16:1-3) and Dr. Luke joined them in Troas (Acts 16:10). All of them moved into Lydia's house. Later though, the account mentioned only Paul and Silas (Acts 16:40). The scripture however implied that all four men entered Europe after being forbidden work in Asia. Imagine the cost of feeding them daily.

Moreover, these men came from different regions of the Roman Empire and therefore had different dietary needs. Obviously, Paul and Silas who were Jews would have some dietary restrictions. Hostesses normally work hard to please their guests, so one could imagine Lydia's efforts to meet every guest's dietary needs on a regular basis. The missionaries had no fixed agenda for Lydia to be certain of when they would leave town. She had to plan under the direction of God and be wise about purchasing bulk groceries for specific cuisines. I wonder how she managed the day to day domestic decisions in addition to her other responsibilities, but she did it anyway.

Time

Lydia would have reorganized her commitments to have time for her guests. She would set a special time aside to spend with the missionaries on regular basis possibly to talk about the things of God and develop a closer relationship among themselves. Sharing their cultural differences in the love of

God, strengthening each other and developing a powerful bond that helped in reaching the city of Philippi for Christ.

Lack of privacy

Lydia would also be faced with lack of privacy. Knowing people from a distance would not be the same as living in a close range. Attitudes and habits otherwise hidden become exposed. Even though every person has a weakness, a hostess' would become more glaring.

In the case of couples, solid marriages could crack as a result of guests manipulating husband and wife. And the unfortunate partner would have to live with the aftermath which could range from character assassination to cancerous bitterness. Wives would mostly end up as the unfortunate ones because they usually oversee the domestic needs and thus have more contact with guests. Woe betides such a woman if she came from cultural backgrounds that believe in communal hospitality. Meanwhile, guests would not pause to think that it took two people to make the home.

Despite these potential setbacks, Lydia, was able to deal with the issue of privacy and lived transparently for her guests.

Lydia offered what she could

Lydia evaluated herself and offered what she could to the missionaries. She knew that she had the means to host them for a long period of time without their financial contribution. She also knew that she would have no problem tolerating their religious beliefs. And she was willing to be available to them whenever they needed her.

People should be sincere about how much they could offer before they embark on hospitality, otherwise their services would end in sadness. For an example, a hostess could offer a space for guests who may stay longer, but require that they buy their own meals. Others could simply provide regular meals but not shelter.

Women must be comfortable with their choices and not be compelled to take on something beyond their strength, influenced by cultural or misinterpretations of scripture. If one time hosting a meal or an overnight sleep-over is all that a woman can do, it should be fine. For neither Christian love nor cultural constraints should force women, otherwise after offering hospitality they would complain bitterly like the person described in this scripture:

> *Do not eat the food of a stingy man; do not crave his delicacies;*
> *for he is the kind of man who is always thinking about the cost.*
> *"Eat and drink," he says to you, but his heart is not with you.*

> **Proverbs 23:6-7**

Not all Christian women may have the opportunity to host missionaries like Lydia did, but many could baby-sit for needy families. Or listen to bereaved persons and offer comfort.

Like the missionaries who had nothing to give in return materially to Lydia's kindness, biblical hospitality is supposed to reach out to those who cannot return it.

Reflect on these:

1. What motivates you to offer hospitality to others?

2. This week practice some kind of hospitality to a stranger or someone you have not spent time with before?

A wise servant will rule over a disgraceful son.

Proverbs 17:2a

CHAPTER NINE

LYDIA, A LEADER WITHOUT TITLE

I thought about Lydia as an untitled leader after the biblical survey I did showed that her name appeared just two times in the Bible. Both in the book of Acts chapter 16 and recorded without any title.

Lydia was neither a deaconess as Phoebe (Romans 16:1) nor a prophetess as Huldah (2Kings 22:14). Yet, she was positively mentioned in the Bible, in a way that placed her as the bedrock for the European Christian church.

Lydia's love for God translated into seeking the welfare of others who equally believed in Him including the bearers of the gospel. Lydia served in a productive way to benefit those who received her services. And affected change in the life of the few women at the riverside, her household members and the missionaries. This gesture multiplied into the birth of a whole church in Philippi.

Lydia as *a mover and shaker* affected the lives of people around her as a charismatic leader. She was a leader in her own right without a title and this chapter is devoted to how she played this special role.

Lydia's leadership

I have been wondering about how the women's prayer group at the Philippian riverside started since I begun writing this book. Lydia was part, and from her story it would not be surprising if she started it, even though she did not claim ownership. Her social connections could easily provide a natural network of women to form the group. What she needed to do was to invite few believing customers who would bring others.

Most likely, Lydia organised these women, who believed in the same God and were residing in Philippi. It was a natural thing to do as a believer in a new place. The first time I lived in an apartment building in Canada, I went round looking for other Christians in the building I could pray with regularly. The women who responded to Lydia's influence might not be all immigrants, from the same social class and converts of the Jewish God. But they all benefited in the end as their fellowship became a vibrant church.

The women's group was just the tip of the iceberg considering how Lydia influenced her household members to accept the Christian faith by leading them to listen to the gospel. She made it possible for them to have time for the things of God and created the atmosphere for practice.

Lydia's handling of the Christian missionaries was the crown of her unique leadership style. She could understand their message of salvation from the beginning and did not waste time to make it accessible to others. But she also managed to move the missionaries into her house before they started the first church of Europe. Lydia did her homework as any good leader would and evaluated the situation. Observing that the missionaries needed domestic and social support, she developed a plan to reach out to them without taking the credit for herself.

Lydia had the discernment and could reason that this band of Jewish men, headed by an ex-Pharisee (Paul), would not accept hospitality from a gentile, single woman. She therefore applied diplomacy and argued on the basis of common faith in God through salvation and baptism in the Lord Jesus Christ.

The beauty in her strategy was that, Lydia knew that the missionaries could not refuse a gift that came in the name of the Lord Jesus Christ. So she used that medium. Smart woman!

Often people think leaders should be people who have impressive academic achievements, professional excellence and are famous. And many consider age and experience as indicators of good leadership. Using only these criteria will not only be inappropriate but also short-sighted. Because impressive qualifications, fame and excellence at work do not necessarily give a person the ability to influence people for the better. In fact, some women step over others to excel in what they do and achieve success through dubious means. Age and experience on the other hand may not apply to many people who neither learn nor apply gains from their years.

However, women who fear God and positively combine some of this qualities—academic and professional excellence, fame, and years of experience, love and understanding—would excel in leading without official titles.

Influence is a single vibrant quality every leader must possess. Positive influence like Lydia exhibited comes only from understanding God and respecting his creation.

The power of positive influence

Positive influence affects lives for the better and could be measured by the change that occurs as a result of contact with others.

Lives that otherwise were aimless develop a purpose; individuals stuck in a place move on and improve the quality of their lives.

Women, who genuinely want to see the kingdom of God established in the hearts of people, will affect people's lives for good, not necessarily in a spectacular way but through simple everyday kindness, concern and affection. Our world needs love and understanding than truckloads of food and medicine.

For a smile brightens the face and lightens the burdens of the heart.

Sadly though, several Christians want to have positions and titles to be able to function as positive influence on others. Some Christian leaders have also become insecure and controlling that they cannot acknowledge people's gifts and talents and allow them to flourish in the Church. In such a milieu, one wonders if it will be possible to see God work through people with positive influence at all.

But it is possible.

Just as Lydia did, Christian women need no positions and titles to lead. Simply identify a need and work positively to bring a change in that area with the help of God. It could be providing consistent encouragement to children, or making regular telephone contacts to isolated individuals, sharing a smile or patiently listening to hurting individuals and visiting shut-ins. The positive change that will result from these activities cannot be imagined.

Remember, nothing is small in the sight of God as He can use just a gift of a cup of water to a stranger to bring about change in the person's life. The good things people do in secret without credit receive approval from God.

Many great contributors in life were silent leaders who had no titles. Consider the mothers and wives of people like John Wesley, D.L. Moody, and contemporaries like Billy Graham; women who nurtured these men who had contributed immensely to Christianity. The efforts (sometimes sacrifices) of these women turned these ordinary men into great men of God.

In this same category are school teachers, whose positive influence on aimless children structured them into meaningful adults and good citizens of society. Consider donors who contributed to ensure that the hungry were fed, and the sick healed in war-torn countries. And countless single mothers who toiled day and night to raise children. They all led without recognition and are unsung heroes, who made the world a better place.

Influential women think about the joy they will bring to families and society in general as they commit to their responsibilities.

Lydia's Christian leadership

In addition to Lydia's influence, she willingly served others to bring about change as the Bible clearly requires of Christian leaders. Service as an attribute complements influence perfectly. In Mark 9:33-35, Jesus taught that those who want to lead must serve and He demonstrated this by washing the feet of his disciples (John 13:1-8). "The basin and the towel" has since become the Christian symbol of leadership. An image of servitude and humility: qualities that every Christian leader should aspire to have.

Serving our families, members of the church and the community at large in different capacities are all instances of leading without a title. A Bible school principal I knew once explained this concept to student pastors that: "anyone who wants to be a deacon must first learn to dig." Literally, digging involves manual work. And until people are willing to take the tools to dig, and dirty themselves, they cannot lead as deacons. The purpose of service is also to effect change and when Christians willingly serve others, they stop satisfying personal egos. They become like John the Baptist, and they seek the increase of others above their own.

In Christian terms, leading is not a position as it is in the secular sense. Rather, it is offering service for the benefit of others.

Lydia's example shows that women everywhere can make a positive difference.

She was proactive and did not follow the exploitation of the times nor manipulated the missionaries for her benefit. She simply initiated change as she saw fit.

Lydia offered the missionaries opportunity to concentrate on preaching the gospel, while she took care of their domestic needs. That is the difference between many titled egoistic Christian leaders and simple untitled women leaders like Lydia.

Woman, you are a leader, because you have it within you to effect positive change. So go make a difference!

Reflect on These:

1. Think of a way that you can lead by serving a person.

2. Select someone (family member, friend, colleague or anybody in your life) and plan to influence in a special and positive way.

3. Some suggestions for service and positive influence:

   •   Spend time with a lonely person.

   •   Encourage and help someone to look for a job - go through the yellow pages or the internet together, help with the telephone calls to agencies.

   •   Help someone look for a school. Help to fill out admission forms.

   •   Help someone access community resources.

   •   Spend time with someone hurting.

   •   Pray for someone.

   •   Give a smile freely to people you meet today.

She is clothed with strength and dignity; she can laugh at the days to come.

Proverbs 31:25

CHAPTER TEN

LYDIA, THE LIBERATED WOMAN

The story of Lydia reveals one woman's liberation from social and religious constraints on womanhood.

In the part one of this book, her character study from the brief biblical narrative presented a woman who feared God and lived in a patriarchal society. Part two showed her distinct qualities that were awesome for a woman who lived in the Roman Empire in a Roman colony city, in the New Testament times. Combining the two parts of this book, Lydia strongly stands out as a woman who exhibited a liberated life before her time.

Two thousand years after Lydia's story was written, the revolution of women's liberation hit the world and women has since the last century been fighting for equality with men in all spheres of life.

Women are now determined to take their active part in society and this trend has revolutionalised the thinking of society in general. These contemporary expressions of women's liberation may not be acceptable in several Christian circles. Yet, in spite of it, Lydia's story brings its own distinct concept of women's liberation that is worth knowing.

This concluding chapter is dedicated to Lydia's liberation, but it is important to learn about what the term actually implies.

A brief look at women's liberation

There are many theories on women's liberation. Equality with men in terms of; economics, social standing and politics are the main arguments. These have been distorted on different levels bordering on an acute hatred for men. Meanwhile some women criticize major contenders for the fight for equality with men as hypocrites. That these are women from the privileged background who have no clue of the experiences of under-privileged women of colour, class and culture. Extreme theories include the all-sufficiency of women with no need for men. To the Christian woman however, these are not the issues. In fact, some of these views will border on heresy, because the Bible teaches that women are created as men's helpers. So women need men in their lives.

Due to these different views given to the concept of women's liberation it is not a popular phrase for many Christians. But Christian women should be open-minded as they read Lydia's story and especially this chapter. Lydia redefines the concept and gives it a new meaning.

In Lydia's story a liberated woman recognizes her original state of being (as God intended for her) as against the dictates of society.

Lydia's source of liberation

Lydia's genuine fear in God was the beginning of her journey into liberation. In those patriarchal times, she freely controlled her life without fear because she knew her strength came from a solid source. This source was the ultimate truth that brought her freedom. The Lord Jesus Christ said:

Then you will know the truth, and the truth will set you free. **John 8:32**

God is Truth and those who trust in Him should live a life of liberation.

Lydia could dare to be different and challenge the status quo. She worshipped a strange God in Roman Philippi even though she knew she could attract persecution from the high society she worked with that considered Caesar as God. She knew the risk that she was taking but she also knew the mighty God she believed in. Her simple assurance was that her God would be able to take her through whatever difficulties that would come her way as she pursued her dreams.

It is important to remember the source of Lydia's liberation as not from female aggressive politics with males but simple acknowledgement of God as sovereign over her life.

Lydia's exhibition of her liberation

Although Lydia was one of the good women mentioned in the Bible, her story showed her as a very independent and highly determined woman. She exhibited liberation in the things she did including entering into a lucrative competitive business and heading her household without a man.

Lydia was able to stand firm as a woman of substance, who was not threatened by competitive men in her line of business. Her career in the purple cloth industry would be normally considered as beyond the scope of a woman. But genuine faith in God gave her the confidence and assurance that all things were possible.

It is often said of women in some line of work as; 'she is doing a man's job' or 'that is not a woman's responsibility.' Women in job positions traditionally reserved for men face this challenge everyday. Most likely, the same was said about Lydia.

Moreover, women were not expected to be heads of households. Lydia was and it wasn't as if her household was made up of just her and her child. From what was presented in the Bible story, she headed a big household with servants. Women in the Roman Empire did not normally own property, they could only own property through their husbands and yet Lydia owned a household. Only an independent woman could live like that in those days. Lydia was neither disobedient to God nor defiant to the laws of society by assuming those roles. She simply did what was pleasing to God and right for her at the time.

Consider the example of a woman CEO who is a mother or a hard-working woman who is trying to become the first president of a super-power. Even fellow women sometimes join in to undermine the efforts of these hard working women. And though people consider their choices unwomanly or against the norm, there is no written law against these aspirations.

Throughout history, women who aspired to live up to their potential had to cross societal barriers and climb those difficult mountains. Lydia surely crossed it smoothly with her faith in God. And showed by her life that women had the potential to do any job at any time and anywhere the Lord might place them. She neither succumbed to the wishes of society nor followed its dictates that made no sense. When Paul came into contact with her, he made no effort to stop her from her roles. Lydia simply went on living her life *unstoppable*.

What liberated women do

Like Lydia, liberated women have a sense of who they are and do not give in to things that will set them back from realizing their potential. They have characteristics that lead them to success. I am going to list a few below:

1. Liberated women put abstract ideas of liberation into action in productive ways that benefit them and the general society.

2. Liberated women embrace hard work. They persevere in the face of challenges, bearing in mind that their goals would be achieved only through hard work.

3. Liberated women focus on their goals. they work towards completing the assignments they have set for themselves. Take my example. About twenty years ago, I dreamt of writing this book, I could not do so because I just toyed with the idea and stopped whenever I faced difficulties. When I finally decided to publish it, I have worked tirelessly—nights and weekends, amidst my busy schedule—till its completion.

Every dream is attainable with God and determination. Liberated women do not compare their situation with others or let their pace worry them. They think in terms of better move with the pace of a tortoise to finish the race than that of the hare and miss out. They know that even if they are going at a slow pace they are still bound to succeed.

Determined women following the example of Lydia should note that like most things, life is a process that develops over time.

A general call for action

This final call is to women who have read this story of Lydia.

Don't languish in lack of self-esteem and measure up to other people's expectations. And don't be afraid to be different. Examine your life and make plans if you haven't. If you have a plan already review it, knowing that there are things in your life that only you can do.

Move on and realize your dreams.

The story goes that; a thirsty donkey brought to the riverside to drink would remain thirsty if it does not open its mouth to take the water.

Nobody can dream for you. You need to dream for yourself and move to realize it. Lydia took absolute control over her faculties as a liberated woman. She tactfully exerted appropriate power over her household to prevent servants rebelling against her headship as a woman.

It is true that society has been and is still patriarchal in many ways. The church as an institution is not innocent. Yet, a woman who knows the Lord can confidently live a liberated life in the face of all these difficulties and maintain her God-given authority in all spheres of life.

Remember always that Lydia never fitted in. She stood out as the *woman from Thyatira*.

Reflect on these:

1. Take your developed life plan; begin to work with your set goals within flexible time frames. Set some dates.

2. Do not rush, but actively work at a consistent pace as you keep in mind that

All things are possible with the Lord.

CONCLUSION

LYDIA AND THE CHURCH OF PHILIPPI

The missionaries had good grounds to plant the seed of the gospel and it grew to become the church in Philippi. Paul and Silas were jailed for casting out demons from a slave girl. This girl made her owners wealthy because she possessed a spirit by which she could predict the future (Acts 16:19). Imagine what a scandal that would have caused in the Philippian society for a person like Lydia to be associated with such a slave girl.

Lydia would be mocked and could be persecuted as the friend of the strange missionaries who were collapsing business in the city by converting idol worshippers to Christ. But it did not stop Lydia from having close links with the missionaries. She continued to be their hostess for as long as they remained in the city of Philippi.

When Paul and Silas were released from prison after sharing the gospel with their jailor who converted to the Christian faith, they returned to Lydia's home. There they met with the other brethren of the first European Christian Church. The church grew to have diverse members. The early members were Lydia and her household, the converted slave girl, and the jailor and his household. Most likely, the church continued to meet at Lydia's home even after Paul and Silas left.

The church that met in Lydia's home gradually grew to be the Philippian Church which was so dear to Paul. They received the lovely letter from Paul titled "Philippians" in the New Testament. One remarkable thing about this church was its distinct characteristic of *giving*. The church continued showing kindness to Paul and other believers just as Lydia, its first convert exemplified. They sent Paul help during his difficult times (2Corinthians 8:1-3).

Another thing worth noting in this church was how God introduced women into the founding of the first European

Christian church before He opened the door to men. Lydia, the women praying by the riverside, and even the slave girl became members of the church before God in His wisdom brought in men like the jailor and his household (Acts 16:23-34).

Philippi was God's expression that it was time for women to come out from hiding. Since God had a special purpose for the work at Philippi, He uniquely positioned Lydia to be the medium to show the world about women's place in the history of the Christian church.

Although Lydia's name was never mentioned again in the Bible after Acts chapter 16, and nothing was written about her end, her story has been influencing lives since the first century.

Meet the biblical author of the story of Lydia: Dr. Luke

We are fortunate to get the original story of Lydia from a Christian who found it appropriate to document events of the time. The writer of the story of Lydia joined Paul and the missionaries at Troas where Paul received the *Macedonian call.* The scripture give the account as follows:

> *So they passed by Mysia and went down to Troas.*
> *During the night Paul had a vision of a man of*
> *Macedonia standing and begging him, "Come over to*
> *Macedonia and help us." After Paul had seen the vision,*
> ***we*** *got ready at once to leave for Macedonia, concluding*
> *that God had called* ***us*** *to preach the gospel to them.*
> **Acts 16:8 (*emphasis, mine*)**

It is important to give this Christian author a place in this book. He was called Luke and was a doctor. Paul referred to him as *our dear friend Luke, the doctor* (Colossians 4:14).

Doctor Luke was and is popularly accepted by Bible scholars as the writer of the book of Acts, and the gospel of

Luke, for which Acts was a sequel (Luke 1:3, Acts 1:1). Dr. Luke introduced himself as part of the missionary team at Troas in the famous *we* and *us* pronouns in the book of Acts as shown in the scripture quoted above. The change from *they* to *we* and *us* indicated that, the writer of Acts has now joined the team.

Interestingly, very little was known about Dr. Luke. And most of what was known was deduced from his writings. Some Scholars speculate that Dr. Luke was a native of Troas because he joined the team there. Others think that he was the symbolic Macedonian man in Paul's vision. But he could have met Paul in one of the towns he ministered to in Galatia or a native of Palestine. At any rate, he joined the group in Troas and became a member of Paul's missionary team to Europe.

Dr. Luke remained a faithful member of Paul's missionary team until Paul died (2Timothy 4:11 and Philemon 24).

EPILOGUE

I thank God for the strength to complete this book. It has been over twenty years since I developed interest in the character Lydia and started to write about her. In my late teens, I related to her as a young woman very keen on serving God without compromises. I admired Lydia as an independent, successful, career single woman. She was my model of a liberated woman and I particularly liked the fact that she drew her strength from faith in God.

Now as a grown-up woman with a husband and children, I relate to Lydia as a woman of substance, able to manage all her responsibilities. I admire Lydia's distinct quality as a single woman, head of household. She is my biblical model for Christian single mothers. The role these women play in raising citizens for society is often overlooked. And since the church usually works within a paradigm of two parent family (husband and wife), single women, and single mothers are often ignored and left behind. Lydia's story distinctly brings their situation to light. God, who enabled Lydia to live a successful single life, is the same today. He continues to enable those who seek Him.

In the future, Lydia will continue to be my model of a liberated woman. Her uniqueness in combining spiritual empowerment from devotion to God with secular, career-oriented independence is classic. She fits the description of today's superwoman and the purpose driven woman. Lydia provides adequately what every Christian woman needs for motivation and shows that women could draw from within themselves, that God-given potential, to become what they were created to be.

Lydia drives home the fact that there is nothing wrong with managing a career and family responsibilities as a Christian woman. She mastered both worlds: the private and the public, and still had time for the things of God. At this age and time, when God is using women to make breakthroughs all over the world, Christian women should not remain behind. It is our God-given mandate to be men's helpers, which includes work beside them in all spheres of life.

This book is written to encourage Christian women of our time. The sky is the limit for what God can do with us. We should pursue what is on our hearts in the fear of the Lord; be it academic development, career or business, we should go for it wholeheartedly. If your choice is to stay home and raise your children, it is equally great! Let no one look down upon you. Making it in a male dominated culture as a woman is not easy, and to listen to destructive criticisms will be detrimental to success.

If Lydia was able to make it in the First Century, then nothing should prevent the woman of the Twenty-first century.

Remember always though that wisdom, blessings and prosperity come from God. For the fear of God is what made Lydia a super woman of her day, not her personal efforts.

I conclude this book by once again presenting you the first Christian feminist, the first Christian convert of Europe, the superwoman, LYDIA.

GENERAL BIBLIOGRAPHY

1. Drage, Hale, Rosemary. (2004). Understanding Christianity. Duncan Baird Publishers: London.

2. Ehrlich, Carl, S. (2004).Understanding Judaism. Duncan Baird Publishers: London.

3. Encyclopaedia Britannica (1960), Volume 11; Volume 14; (pp.515-516); Volume 17; (p. 726); Volume 19;.William Benton Publisher: Chicago.

4. Gardiner, D. Paul. (1995). The Complete Who's Who in the Bible; Zondervan Publishing House, Michigan, USA (p. 428).

5. Lendering, Jona. Online article on Lydia (http://www.livius.org/lu-lz/lydia.html).

6. Macarthur, John. (2005). Twelve Extraordinary Women. Thomas Nelson: Nashville, Tennessee, (pp.187-197).

7. The Atlas of the Classical World, Ancient Greece and Ancient Rome (1997). Stoddart Publishing: Canada

8. The Atlas of the Bible Lands (1997). Stoddart Publishing: Canada.

9. Vine, W., E. (1984). Vine's Complete Expository Dictionary of old and New Testament Words. Thomas Nelson Publishers: Nashville.

10. Wiersbe, Warren, W. (1992). Wiersbe Expository Outlines On the New Testament. Chariot Victor Publishing: Colorado Springs, USA. (Pp.320-321).

11. Viening, Edward. (1969). The Zondervan Topical Bible. Zondervan Publishing House: Grand Rapids, Michigan. USA.